W9-CXW-732

Watch It Grow

Goldfish

by Martha E. H. Rustad

Consulting editor: Gail Saunders-Smith, PhD

Consultant: Ronald M. Coleman, Assistant Professor
Department of Biological Sciences
California State University, Sacramento

Capstone
press®

Mankato, Minnesota

J
597.4
RUS

Pebble Books are published by Capstone Press,
151 Good Counsel Drive, P.O. Box 669, Mankato, Minnesota 56002.
www.capstonepress.com

 Books published by Capstone Press are manufactured with paper
containing at least 10 percent post-consumer waste.

Library of Congress Cataloging-in-Publication Data
Rustad, Martha E. H. (Martha Elizabeth Hillman), 1975–
  Goldfish / by Martha E. H. Rustad.
  p. cm. — (Pebble books. Watch it grow)
  Includes bibliographical references and index.
  Summary: "Simple text and photographs present the life cycle of goldfish" —
Provided by publisher.
  ISBN: 978-1-4296-3309-3 (library binding)
  ISBN: 978-1-4296-3856-2 (paperback)
  1. Goldfish — Life cycles — Juvenile literature. I. Title. II. Series.
QL638.C94R87 2010
597'.484 — dc22   2009004919

Note to Parents and Teachers

The Watch It Grow set supports national science standards related
to life science. This book describes and illustrates goldfish. The
images support early readers in understanding the text. The
repetition of words and phrases helps early readers learn new
words. This book also introduces early readers to subject-specific
vocabulary words, which are defined in the Glossary section. Early
readers may need assistance to read some words and to use the
Table of Contents, Glossary, Read More, Internet Sites, and Index
sections of the book.

Table of Contents

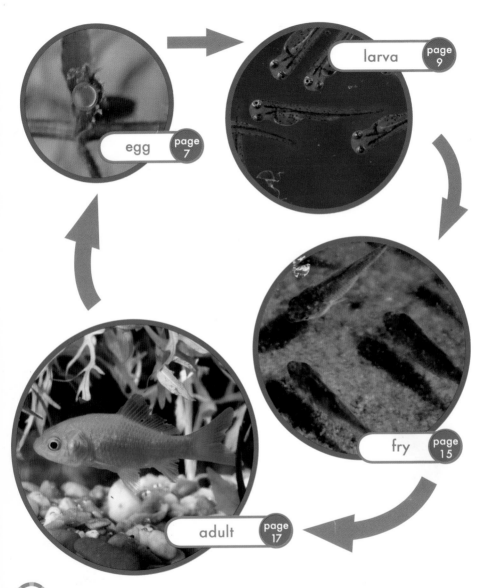

larva page 9

egg page 7

fry page 15

adult page 17

Metamorphosis

Goldfish change
as they grow
from egg to adult.
This change is called
metamorphosis.

egg

From Egg to Larva

Goldfish begin life as eggs
in a lake or stream.
A female goldfish lays
hundreds of tiny eggs.
The eggs stick to plants.

Goldfish larvae hatch
after about one week.
They hatch faster
in warm water
than cold water.

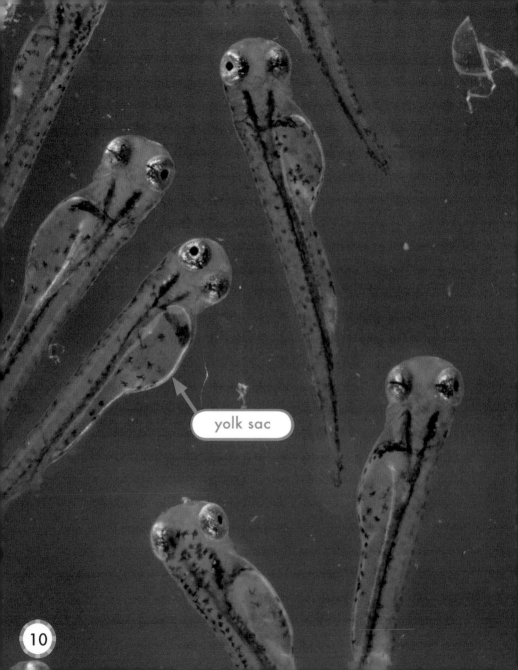

yolk sac

Goldfish larvae are small.
They cannot swim.
They feed off a yolk sac
on their bellies.

Goldfish larvae grow fins, wide tails, and scales. They breathe through gills.

From Larva to Fry

Goldfish larvae become fry
after about two weeks.
Fry can swim and find food.
They eat plants, insects,
and small animals.

From Fry to Adult

Goldfish become adults
when they begin to breed.
Females lay eggs.
The life cycle begins again.

Wild goldfish live in lakes and slow streams or rivers. They can be orange, gray, dark green, or white.

Goldfish grow all their lives.
Some goldfish grow up
to 2 feet (.6 meter) long.
They live as long as
15 years.

Glossary

breed — to mate and produce young; female goldfish lay eggs and male goldfish fertilize the eggs.

fry — the third stage of a goldfish's life; a fry looks like a small adult goldfish.

gill — a body part used to take oxygen from water; fish live underwater and use gills to breathe.

hatch — to break out of an egg

larva — the second stage of a goldfish's life

metamorphosis — the physical changes that some animals go through as they develop from eggs to adults

scale — one of the small, thin plates that covers the body of a fish

yolk sac — a small pouch attached to the body of a fish larva; the yolk inside the sac is the larva's only food.

Read More

Burstein, John. *Goldfish.* Slim Goodbody's Inside Guide to Pets. Pleasantville, N.Y.: Gareth Stevens, 2008.

MacAulay, Kelley and Bobbie Kalman. *Goldfish.* Pet Care. New York: Crabtree, 2005.

Internet Sites

FactHound offers a safe, fun way to find Internet sites related to this book. All of the sites on FactHound have been researched by our staff.

Here's all you do:

Visit *www.facthound.com*

FactHound will fetch the best sites for you!

Index

Word Count: 159
Grade: 1
Early-Intervention Level: 21

Editorial Credits

Katy Kudela, editor; Alison Thiele, designer; Marcie Spence, media researcher

Photo Credits

Capstone Press/Karon Dubke, cover (goldfish), 1, 4 (bottom left), 6, 16
Courtesy of Rasika Ambepitiyage, cover (egg), 4 (top left), 6 (inset)
Getty Images Inc./Paul Zahl/National Geographic, cover (larvae), 4 (top right), 8, 10
iStockphoto/fotandy, 20
Oranda/Flickr, 12
Photograph provided by Jo Fisher, UK., 4 (bottom right), 14
Visuals Unlimited/Walt Anderson, 18